WORLD RELIGIONS
HINDUISM

BY NATALIE M. ROSINSKY

Content Adviser:
Anantanand Rambachan, Professor and Chair,
Religion Department, St. Olaf College

Reading Adviser:
Alexa L. Sandmann, Ed.D., Professor of Literacy,
College and Graduate School of Education,
Health, and Human Services, Kent State University

Compass Point Books
151 Good Counsel Drive
P.O. Box 669
Mankato, MN 56002-0669

 This book was manufactured with paper containing
at least 10 percent post-consumer waste.

Photographs ©: Alamy: Dinodia Images 18–19, Louise Batalla Duran 29, 31,
Nikolai Ignatiev 7, World Religions Photo Library 24–25; AP Photo: John Amis 42;
Dreamstime: Sunny_13 38–39; Getty Images: AFP/John MacDougall 33, AFP/Sam
Panthaky 28, Liaison/Netphoto/Pablo Bartholomew 4–5, National Geographic/
Martin Gray 14; iStockphoto: AlexFox 27, Anantha Vardhan 15, Anna Ceglinska
23, Gina Smith 32, Luciano Mortula 21, TheFinalMiracle 34, Vikram Raghuvanshi
cover; Shutterstock: Andrey Plis 22, Dmitry Rukhlenko 13, Ine Beerten 36–37,
maga (background texture) 4, 10, 18, 29, 38, 46, 47, Mariya Sverlova 10–11,
Vladimir Wrangel (carving design element) cover (top & bottom), back cover (top),
1, 45, sidebars throughout.

Editor: Brenda Haugen
Designers: Ashlee Suker and Bobbie Nuytten
Media Researcher: Svetlana Zhurkin
Art Director: LuAnn Ascheman-Adams
Creative Director: Joe Ewest
Editorial Director: Nick Healy
Managing Editor: Catherine Neitge
Cartographer: XNR Productions, Inc.

Library of Congress Cataloging-in-Publication Data
Rosinsky, Natalie M. (Natalie Myra)
Hinduism / by Natalie M. Rosinsky.
    p. cm.—(World religions)
Includes index.
ISBN 978-0-7565-4238-2 (library binding)
1. Hinduism—Juvenile literature. I. Title. II. Series.
BL1203.R685 2009
294.5—dc22
                                        2009009349

Visit Compass Point Books on the Internet at *www.compasspointbooks.com*
or e-mail your request to *custserv@compasspointbooks.com*

Table of Contents

Chapter One
"SINS ... WASHED AWAY HERE"

In January 2001, about 20,000 people waded into the Ganges River in Allahabad, India. In the chilly dawn hours, the water was icy cold. Yet even families with small children and elderly grandparents eagerly waited their turn to plunge into the sacred river.

Crowds covered almost every inch of its sandy bank. Some people laughed and spoke with excitement in their voices. Others stood in silent prayer or crouched down to place colorful flowers and other offerings in the water. They felt joy at taking part in this grand ritual of their religion, Hinduism. As one person explained, "The sins that we have created are washed away here."

This ritual is part of the Maha Kumbh Mela, the Grand Pitcher Festival, which takes place every 12 years. During the six-week festival, millions of devout Hindus travel across India to reach this holy spot, where the Ganges and Yamuna rivers meet. It's said that divine beings once fought demons here for a liquid that gives eternal life. Hindus from other countries also go on the pilgrimage. It has become the largest gathering on Earth. In 2001 Indian officials estimated that 30 million people took part in the Maha Kumbh Mela. The gathering was so vast that it could be seen by satellites in space.

Poor people as well as rich ones took part in the ritual. Some had traveled to the Ganges on foot, wearing threadbare clothes and carrying their belongings in cloth bundles. Others came in ox-drawn

A holy man wore the crescent moon of the Hindu god Shiva in his hair during a Maha Kumbh Mela festival.

The Caste System

For thousands of years, a social-class system called the caste system structured the lives of Hindus. Traditionally people were born into their caste and stayed in it all their lives. The highest caste—the Brahmin caste—consisted of priests. Warriors and kings formed the next caste. Merchants were the third class. The lowest caste was occupied by laborers and servants. Although the Indian government outlawed the caste system in 1949, some of its effects still exist in Indian society. Neighborhood clusters, family wealth or position, and people's attitudes sometimes still reflect the banned caste system. But this is changing, especially in urban areas. Outside India the caste system plays an even smaller part in the lives of Hindus.

carts, on horses, or on overcrowded buses and trains. Still others arrived in sleek cars or jet planes. They wore expensive clothing and brought along computers, cameras, and cell phones.

People rowed across the Yamuna River to the festival site in Allahabad.

People from all castes in Hindu society were represented in the crowd. The first arrivals for this festival, though, included holy men. Some were *sadhus*, who dedicate their lives to Hinduism. They could be identified by their bare bodies streaked with ash and their long, matted hair. Other groups included wise men called gurus, who wore traditional orange robes. They rang bells or chanted as they read aloud from sacred Hindu works. Before and after dipping into the frigid Ganges, many people listened to these holy words.

The Maha Kumbh Mela festival is typical of Hinduism, the oldest organized religion, because of its size, location, and inclusion of people of all kinds. Hinduism's first believers lived in what is now India, and it's the third-largest faith in the world. About 13 percent of the

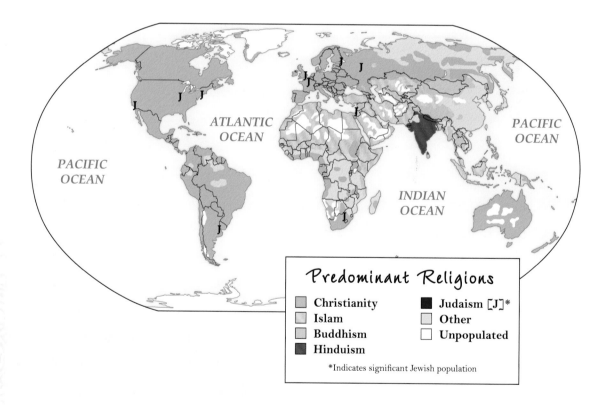

ATLANTIC OCEAN

PACIFIC OCEAN

PACIFIC OCEAN

INDIAN OCEAN

Predominant Religions

- ☐ Christianity
- ☐ Islam
- ☐ Buddhism
- ☐ Hinduism
- ■ Judaism [J]*
- ☐ Other
- ☐ Unpopulated

*Indicates significant Jewish population

The World's Hindus

There are about 900 million Hindus in the world, and about 98 percent of them live in India. About 80 percent of India's population is Hindu. Other countries with large numbers of Hindus are Nepal, Indonesia, Bangladesh, Pakistan, Sri Lanka, Malaysia, South Africa, Trinidad, Guyana, and Surinam. The United States has nearly 1.5 million Hindus. Canada and the United Kingdom also have significant numbers of Hindus.

world's population is Hindu. The festival's emphasis on nature and its rite of washing away sin reflect beliefs that are central to this ancient faith.

ORIGINS AND BELIEFS

The set of beliefs known as Hinduism began
about 3500 B.C.E. in the northern region of
what is now India. A civilization flourished
there in the Indus River Valley.
Its remnants are the ruins
of two large cities
called Mohenjo-Daro
and Harappa.

Clay figures found there show that these ancient people worshipped a life-giving mother goddess like Hinduism's Devi. Stone pillars nearby suggest ancient worship of a male life-giving god like Hinduism's Shiva.

Some scholars believe that Aryan tribes from central Asia invaded the Indus Valley around 1500 B.C.E. These invaders brought their own traditions and their own language, which later became Sanskrit, the sacred language of Hinduism. Thus the local religion began to change. But there is significant and often heated debate among scholars about how great an influence Aryan invaders had on the development of Hinduism. Some scholars question the Aryan-invasion theory, saying it reflects a European point of view.

Hinduism's followers acknowledge Brahman as the absolute and boundless God who has many names and is imagined in many forms.

To acknowledge all world religions, Compass Point Books uses new abbreviations to distinguish time periods. For ancient times, instead of B.C., we use B.C.E., which means before the common era. B.C. means before Christ. Similarly, we use C.E., which means in the common era, instead of A.D. The abbreviation A.D. stands for the Latin phrase anno Domini, which means in the year of the Lord, referring to Jesus Christ. Of course not all peoples worship Jesus.

The Hindu god Shiva is also known as Lord of the Dance.

Names for Hinduism

The word *Hindu* comes from an ancient Persian name for the area east of the Indus River—*Sindhu*. Over time Hindu and Hinduism came to describe the inhabitants there and their beliefs. Hindus themselves call their religion Sanatana Dharma. In Sanskrit these words mean "eternal law" or "eternal right way of being."

This God is called by many masculine names, such as Brahma, Vishnu, Shiva, and even feminine names, such as Durga and Kali. Hindus believe that since God is boundless, God's names are limitless. Each region of India has its own favorite name and form for God, but underlying this variety is the understanding that God is one entity who is worshipped in many ways under many names and forms.

Hindus believe God can assume various physical forms on Earth. Vishnu, known to Hindus as God the Sustainer, has 10 forms, which are called avatars. Two of the best-known and best-loved avatars are blue-skinned Krishna and noble Rama. Statues of them and Vishnu are worshipped in Indian temples and homes. Vishnu avatars are also important in some of Hinduism's sacred texts. Vishnu's female counterpart is Lakshmi. She is the goddess of wealth, beauty, and good fortune.

Shiva, the destroyer who also gives life, is sometimes known as Nataraja or Lord of the Dance. His dancing destroys the world and brings it back into existence. It's said that Shiva is married to gentle Parvati. They have two sons, one of whom is the elephant-headed Ganesha, the god of good fortune

Statues of Hindu gods Vishnu and his wife, Lakshmi

and learning. Some Hindus also worship Kali as one of Shiva's wives. She is a fierce warrior goddess but also is known as maternal, tender, and loving.

One form of God very important to some Hindus is Devi, also called Shakti, a creative force similar to Brahma. Worship of Devi might have started with the mother-goddess religion in the ancient cities of Mohenjo-Daro and Harappa.

Stone carvings of the goddess Devi and the serpent form of Shiva

There are thousands of sects of Hinduism, and there may be millions of forms of God. Which form Hindus worship often depends on the community in which they live. Usually everyone in a village worships the same deity. This divine being may be associated with something in the nearby countryside, such as a tree or stream.

Devotion to one deity while respecting the others is typical of practicing Hindus. Still, nearly all Hindus associate certain gods and goddesses with important events or situations. For example, during a Hindu wedding, prayers are said to Kama, the god of pure love, as well as to other deities. People going on a trip pray to Ganesha for good luck.

All Hindus share important spiritual beliefs and goals. They believe that when someone dies, the person's soul lives on and is reincarnated in a new body. Hinduism calls this cycle of birth and rebirth *samsara* and represents it as a wheel.

If someone has lived a good and dutiful life, the person may be reborn into a happy life. Hindus describe good deeds as *dharma*, which means doing one's duty in daily life. Someone who has not followed the path of dharma or has committed evil deeds acquires a spiritual debt. He or she may be reborn into a more difficult life, or even as a nonhuman creature. The influence of good and bad acts in life on reincarnation is called *karma*.

Devout Hindus try to live according to the traditions of dharma described in their sacred texts. They believe that doing so

An Indian farmer works his land. Hindus try to live good, dutiful lives so they will be reborn into better lives.

God in Many Forms

Hindus worship a variety of forms of God on Earth.
Some of the most popular gods and avatars are:

Brahma	known as the creator god
Devi	known as the mother goddess
Ganesha	one of Shiva and Parvati's sons, he is known as the god of good fortune and learning
Kali	fierce warrior goddess also known for her loving, motherly side
Krishna	embodies love and divine joy that destroys all pain and sin
Lakshmi	Vishnu's wife, she is the goddess of wealth, beauty, and good fortune
Parvati	Shiva's wife, known for her gentleness
Rama	depicts the ideal man
Shiva	destroyer who also gives life, also known as Nataraja or Lord of the Dance
Vishnu	preserver and protector of creation

improves their karma, which determines their next reincarnation. The ultimate hope of Hindus is to perfect themselves enough to achieve *moksha*—release from the cycle of birth and rebirth. They believe moksha releases the soul into total closeness with the creative divinity of Brahman.

Besides good deeds and devotion to the gods, Hindus believe that meditating is a way to achieve moksha. Studying Hinduism's sacred texts and observing its rituals is yet another path in the long spiritual journey toward moksha.

World Faiths That Came From Hinduism

Three world religions have sprung from Hinduism, but unlike Hinduism, these faiths have individual founders. Buddhism was founded by Siddhartha Gautama, who lived about 500 B.C.E. in what is now Nepal. He traveled throughout what is now India and became known as the Buddha (Enlightened One) as he spread his beliefs. Also around 500 B.C.E., a man named Mahavira in India spread the religion of Jainism. This religion shares some of the beliefs of Hinduism and Buddhism. In 1469 a man later called Guru Nanak founded the religion of Sikhism. It combines elements of Hinduism with the religion of Islam and is centered in northwestern India.

SACRED TEXTS AND WORSHIP

Hinduism's oldest sacred texts are a collection of hymns, prayers, and songs called the four Vedas (Knowledges). Most scholars believe they were probably written about 1500 B.C.E. These Sanskrit texts include directions for holy rituals and stories about the world's creation.

The Upanishads (meaning in Sanskrit "to sit close by") are the final sections of the Vedas. In the Upanishads, information is told as though religious teachers called gurus were instructing students sitting beside them. The Upanishads teach Hinduism's important beliefs about Brahman, karma, samsara, and moksha.

Brahmin priests, part of the highest caste in traditional Hindu societies, memorized, recited, and translated the Vedas for hundreds of years. Common people—with less education and little knowledge of Sanskrit—also drew upon two other sacred texts for religious inspiration. These appeared during the rise and fall of India's first empire, the Mauryan Empire, between 400 B.C.E. and 400 C.E. These very long poems, called the *Ramayana* and the *Mahabharata*, remain important today for their lessons about Hindu values.

The *Ramayana* was composed around 200 B.C.E. by a poet named Valmiki. It's said that Rama himself—who is one of Vishnu's avatars—told Valmiki his life story. Valmiki used Sanskrit to create this long poem, but the storytellers who memorized it may have translated the *Ramayana* as they told it in various villages. People

The Ramayana *and the* Mahabharata *are long poems that have been passed on from one generation to the next for thousands of years.*

India's Many Languages

The sacred language of Sanskrit unites Hindus within India and throughout the world. More than 400 languages are spoken in India today. Twenty-two local languages are used by regional governments for their official business. The central Indian government officially uses Hindi and English. Hindu beliefs are kept alive by the written Sanskrit language.

eagerly greeted those storytellers, who provided entertainment as well as education. Little in everyday life was as exciting as the events storytellers described.

The *Ramayana* is a dramatic tale of love, loyalty, and duty. Rama is a prince who is banished from his home. He obeys this harsh sentence out of duty. His loyal wife, Sita, and his brother Lakshman accompany him. When Sita is kidnapped by a fierce demon, Rama, with the help of his loyal servant Hanuman, rescues her. Rama and Sita return to their kingdom, where Rama becomes king. In this way, good is shown to triumph over evil. Rama and Sita also model love and faithfulness between husband and wife.

The *Ramayana* has been translated into many lan-

The Ramayana *epic was carved on a wood door inside a temple in Laos.*

guages. It has been performed in plays, filmed as a movie, and even made into a hugely successful TV series. The *Ramayana*—along with the *Mahabharata*—can also be read in popular comic books.

The *Mahabharata* was composed around 200 B.C.E., probably by a wise man named Vyasa. With more than 100,000 verses, it's the world's longest poem. It tells the story of two royal families who struggle to rule the same kingdom. One family tries to cheat the other one, the rightful heirs to the throne.

A statue depicts Hindu god Krishna and Prince Arjuna riding in a chariot.

One section of the *Mahabhrata* is especially popular and well-known. It's called the *Bhagavad Gita* (*The Song of the Lord*). It contains a conversation between the royal prince Arjuna and his charioteer, the god Krishna. They talk about duty in battle and what to do when duty conflicts with feelings. Krishna urges the path of dharma. Heeding Krishna, Arjuna goes into battle and triumphs over his family's enemies. The rightful heirs win the throne. The *Bhagavad Gita* is read frequently by Hindus seeking inspiration and comfort.

Krishna—one of Vishnu's avatars—is one of the most popular of all avatars. Many folktales include stories about Krishna's childhood and the mischief his fun-loving nature caused. Kids especially like hearing those stories. Some of these ancient tales, known as *Puranas*, also feature the god Ganesha. They offer various explanations of how he got his elephant head.

A Hindu family prays before a shrine in Bali, Indonesia.

Sacred texts guide and support the daily prayers that are a vital part of Hinduism. Every morning and night, Hindus recite prayers at a home shrine. This is where they keep their copies of sacred texts. The quiet, separate space has statues or pictures of God in their favorite forms. How lavish or simple a shrine is depends on the family's income. When there are small children living at home, the shrine is usually kept high up— out of the reach of little hands. Once children are old enough to obey rules, the shrine is once again placed in its traditional location, close to the floor and seated worshippers.

Hindus wash before approach-ing their shrine. Then, before praying, they place flowers, fruit, or sweet foods in front of the *murtis* (sacred images). They make these offerings in return for the god's blessings. This worship service is called *puja*.

Some Hindus look to the sun as a powerful and life-giving expression of God and turn toward the sun for morning prayer rituals.

Many Hindus visit temples just to see murtis. This

A girl made an offering at her family's shrine in England.

act of worship is called *darshan*. Many Hindus speak of going to the temple for darshan.

Some Hindus visit a nearby *mandir* (temple) daily, although such attendance is not required. Other Hindus visit mandirs only on special occasions, such as family celebrations or festival days. In a mandir, the murtis are kept in a central shine room. Hindus circle this most sacred area as part of their worship. Many mandirs are elaborately decorated with sculpture and have pyramid-shaped roofs. These represent the mountains of Hindu legends. Other mandirs are simpler.

Entering a mandir, Hindus take off their shoes to show respect for their faith. They may pray. They bring offerings to the murtis in the temple shrine. A priest asks the gods' blessing on these offerings and returns part of them to the worshippers. The priest then marks the forehead of each worshipper. Called a *tilaka* or *bindi*, this small red mark is a sign of the blessing each worshipper received.

Waving light before the icons is a central act of Hindu worship. This act is known as *arati*. The priest asks the sacred images to bless a tray of small, flaming lamps. The tray is then brought to the worshippers, who pass their hands over the blessed flames. This is another way to receive blessings from the gods.

The Most Sacred Word and Symbol

At the beginning and end of all prayers and readings from sacred texts, Hindus chant the word *aum*, sometimes spelled om. For Hindus, this is the most sacred word. Aum is made up of three sounds, which individually represent the gods Brahma, Vishnu, and Shiva. Put together as aum, these sounds stand for the strongest creative force, the god Brahman.

The written symbol for aum is also holy for Hindus. For luck they write it on letters and on exams. Babies even have this symbol traced with honey on their tongues. Hindus may wear jewelry containing an aum.

The symbol for aum

Chief minister of western India's Gujarat state Narendra Modi (left) received blessings from a Hindu priest at a temple in Ahmedabad.

Gurus help Hindus read and study their sacred texts. Some gurus are also temple priests, but many are not. Brahmin priests take care of the mandir's sacred images. During the day, they wash, dress, and offer food to these murtis as honored guests of the temple. Priests lead worship during festivals and also conduct ceremonies to mark the special times in Hindus' lives.

Chapter Four
RITUALS AND FESTIVALS

For a Hindu, rituals and celebrations mark 16 important stages in life. A Brahmin priest helps a family and close friends celebrate these rituals, which are called *samskaras*. Some of these samskaras take place at home, while others are held in the mandir.

A Hindu girl dressed up for her naming ceremony

Hindu Food Customs

Though Hinduism doesn't require a vegetarian diet, many people in India avoid eating meat. Hindus generally eat a vegetarian diet because they believe eating meat causes anger and loss of self-control. They believe that a vegetarian diet expresses non-violence. Hinduism does forbid eating certain meats, particularly beef. Cows are sacred to Hindus because they are vital to life and existence in agricultural India. They are a means of transportation and a source of food products, such as milk and butter.

Many Hindus don't eat any food on certain days of the month and during some festivals. This kind of religious fasting is a tradition in Hinduism.

Many samskaras take place during childhood. A baby's first taste of solid food and formal naming are celebrated with these rituals. Often a family enjoys a feast after an infant's naming ritual. Following Hindu customs, little or no meat is served at this festive meal.

The most important childhood samskara usually takes place between the ages of 8 and 12. That is when Hindu boys are initiated into their religion. There is no similar ceremony for girls. Sometimes called the Sacred Thread ceremony, this samskara marks a boy's coming of age. It's a time for him and his family to feel proud and happy. If he and his parents wish, the boy may now formally study Hinduism with a guru.

During the ceremony, a priest blesses a long, thick, white cotton thread and gives it to the boy. The thread's three strands are to remind the boy of the gods Brahma, Vishnu, and Shiva. The sacred thread is worn over the left shoulder and tied at the waist under the right arm. A boy wears the thread until he is an old man. During

A boy received his sacred thread from his father and a priest.

the ceremony, his father or teacher instructs the now "twice born" young man in Sanskrit prayers. Games, feasts, and gift-giving are also part of this joyous ceremony, which sometimes lasts several days.

A Hindu wedding is another important samskara. The newlyweds are lavishly adorned for this occasion, which lasts several days and involves many prayers, songs, and rituals. In one ritual, the new couple's garments are tied together. They step around a sacred fire as they recite prayers, which include wishes for their

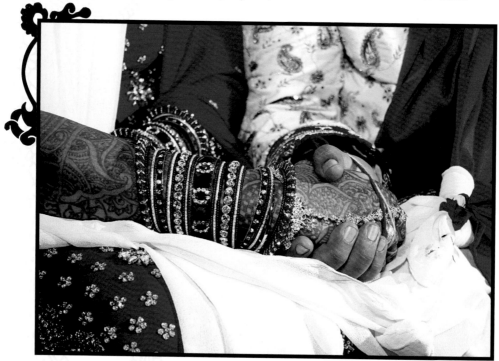

During a wedding ceremony, the hands of a bride and groom are tied together to represent their strong bond to each other.

new life together.

The final samskara is the ceremony held after a Hindu has died. Hindus cremate their dead. Three days after a body has been burned, the ashes are collected and placed in a river. Many Hindus hope to die near the Ganges River or to have their ashes placed in its sacred water. Hindus who live in other countries often arrange to have their ashes scattered in the Ganges.

This sacred river is important in other ways as well. Devout Hindus plan to make at least one pilgrimage to the Ganges. This may take place during a Maha Kumbh Mela, such as the one held in 2001, or at other festivals and rituals celebrated along the Ganges. Many rites take place in the city of Varansari,

Hundreds of thousands of Hindus crowded the banks of the Ganges River during Maha Kumbh Mela.

which is on the river. Sick Hindus bathe in the water by Varansari, hoping to become well. Water from the Ganges is also part of other religious rites and festival celebrations. Many of them are exciting occasions for Hindu children.

Diwali, the Festival of Lights, is an important and joyous religious festival. It's celebrated by Hindus around the globe. Diwali takes place during the Hindu

Many households burn oil lamps at their doorsteps during the Diwali festival.

The Hindu Calendar

The Hindu religious calendar is a lunar one. Months begin with each new moon and end just before a full moon appears. In the current Hindu calendar, the Western year 2009 is the Hindu year 1930–1931.

month of Kartika, which falls in October or November. At this time, Hindus decorate their homes and their mandir with small lamps called *diyas*. These are like the lamps that are said to have welcomed Rama and Sita home after their exile. Families tell or read stories from the *Ramayana*.

Diwali is also a celebration of the Hindu New Year. People often greet one another at this time by saying "Shub Diwali!" This means "Good luck and blessings in the new year!" Hindus also send New Year's cards with good wishes, wear new clothes, and eat lots of good food during Diwali. Sweet treats are especially popular. Many Diwali feasts feature harvest foods. In northern India, Diwali also celebrates a successful harvest.

For Diwali Hindus clean their houses to welcome Lakshmi, the goddess of good fortune. They may decorate doorways with designs called *rangoli* to welcome her. Girls and women sometimes celebrate by using henna paste to decorate their hands with intricate designs called *mehndi*. They enjoy wearing these decorations, which last for about a week before they wash away.

Another festival that young Hindus enjoy is Holi. It's full of messy fun. Holi takes place in February or March. It marks the beginning of spring and honors the legend of Holika. This wicked witch burned in a bonfire when she tried to kill a devoted follower of Krishna. Hindus remember Holika's defeat by burning her image in a bonfire. Many Hindus— especially young ones—throw powdered dyes and water over one another. These pranks, along with singing and dancing, celebrate the mischief and fun that young Krishna is said to have enjoyed. "Happy Holi!" is frequently heard during this playful festival.

Boys were covered with powdered dye during Holi.

Other Hindu festivals include celebrations of the birthdays of Krishna and Ganesha. A nine-day-long festival called Navaratri is devoted to the goddesses Durga, Lakshmi, and Sarasvati, the goddess of the arts.

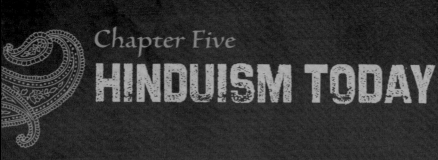

Chapter Five
HINDUISM TODAY

Hinduism continues to grow and adapt to new technology and social change. Around the globe, filmed versions of the *Ramayana* can now be downloaded from the Web. In India the *Mahabharata* has been made into a popular TV series. Hindu taxi drivers in India, the

United States, and other countries display murtis on their dashboards. The drivers pray during their breaks and welcome divine blessings while in traffic, too.

A major change in Indian society has been the organized actions of Dalits, who are Hindus without caste. Once rudely called Untouchables, they traditionally performed the dirtiest, most undesirable jobs. Although the caste system was outlawed in 1949, discrimination against these people still occurs. The caste system has never been universally accepted and practiced by all Hindus. Even though a Dalit named K.R. Narayanan served as India's president from 1997 to 2002, his success didn't end all unfair treatment. In 2001 and again in 2006, nearly 150,000 Dalits protested this discrimination. In massive groups, they converted to Buddhism. The full impact of these protests and conversions remains to be seen.

Modern India also continues to struggle with conflicts between its Hindu majority and Muslim minority. When India became free of British rule in 1947, it divided into mostly Hindu India and mostly Muslim Pakistan. Still, about 10 percent of India's

People wore masks to portray Rama and Sita in a play.

 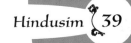

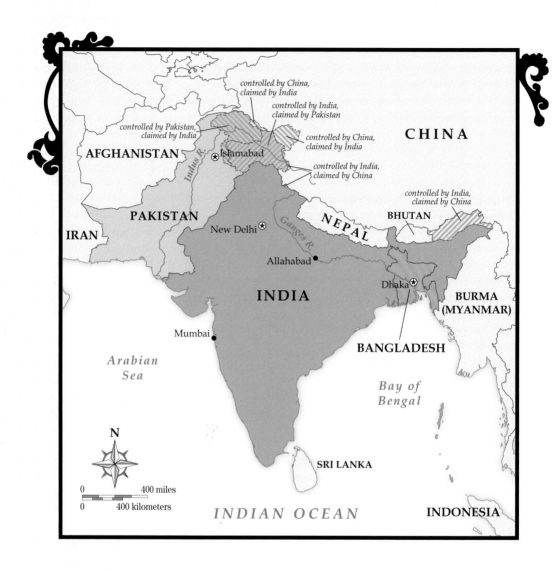

population is Muslim. Thousands have lost either their homes or lives during mob violence stemming from religious differences. A deadly attack in the city of Mumbai by Muslim terrorists occurred in 2008. Political and religious leaders are working to prevent further violence

Invasions and Revolutions

Many invasions have influenced India's Hindu society. The Muslim Mughal Empire controlled northern India from 1526 to 1858. Muslim designs in art and architecture appeared in this region. A less positive effect was the hostile attitude some Muslims and Hindus had toward one another.

British influence began in 1757, with a large trading company called the British East India Company. In 1858 Great Britain created one of its first colonies out of what are today India, Pakistan, and Bangladesh. Led by Mahatma Gandhi, India won its independence in 1947, but the territory was split into the countries of India and Pakistan. Pakistan was separated into West and East Pakistan. In 1971 India supported East Pakistan's war of independence, which resulted in the new nation of Bangladesh.

and promote harmony.

Since 1965 more than a million Hindus have immigrated to the United States. Hindus have built temples in communities across the United States. Sometimes American Hindu families take summer road trips across the country to visit and worship at these temples. It's a new kind of religious pilgrimage.

Hinduism has become part of American society, yet Hindus, as a minority in the United States, still

A volunteer organized a line of Hindus waiting to enter a newly opened temple in Lilburn, Georgia.

encounter prejudice. On September 14, 2000, a Hindu priest for the first time gave the prayer to begin a session of the U.S. House of Representatives. His presence there was later questioned by some extreme Christian groups. Since 1990 the Hindu American community in Edison, New Jersey, has drawn thousands of Hindus to its Navaratri festival. Yet between 1994 and 1997, some non-Hindu residents fought a court battle to end this important rite. Their actions showed that they didn't understand or respect Hindu traditions. U.S. courts, however, upheld the rights of Hindu citizens—along with all other U.S. citizens—to practice their religion. As technology evolves and new generations of Hindus are born, it seems clear that this ancient religion will remain strong.

Influence of Hinduism

Hinduism has inspired people around the world in many ways. One influence can be seen in yoga. Many Hindus use this set of mental and physical exercises to meditate. The practice of yoga in the United States and other countries has become popular as a way to improve health.

The Transcendental Meditation movement, established by Indian guru Maharishi Mahesh Yogi during the 1960s, has also been influential. Celebrities such as The Beatles helped make this movement well-known. Since then some U.S. schools and military organizations have adopted its meditation techniques to reduce stress.

Hinduism has also inspired world leaders and social change. The Hindu leader Mahatma Gandhi used nonviolent resistance to help India achieve independence from Britain. During the American civil rights movement of the 1950s and 1960s, the Reverend Martin Luther King Jr. modeled his successful method of nonviolent resistance on Gandhi's actions.

TIMELINE

3500 B.C.E.   Civilization in the Indus Valley begins, centering on the cities of Mohenjo-Daro and Harappa

1500 B.C.E.   Four Vedas are composed in the Indus Valley

320 B.C.E.   Beginning of the Mauryan Empire, India's first empire, which lasted until 400 C.E.

200 B.C.E.   The *Ramayana* and the *Mahabharata* are composed

1526 C.E.   The Muslim Mughal Empire takes control of northern India; it keeps control through 1858

1757   The British East India Company becomes influential

1858   Britain's governing of India (British Raj) begins

1947   British India is split into India and Pakistan, two separate and independent nations

1949   The caste system is outlawed in India

1997   A Dalit, K. R. Narayanan, is elected president of India

2001   Thirty million people gathered in Allahabad, India, to celebrate Maha Kumbh Mela, making it the largest gathering on Earth

2006   Many Dalits protest discrimination and convert to Buddhism

2008   Muslim terrorists attack citizens and tourists in Mumbai, India, killing more than 80 people

- Tragedy struck during the 1954 Maha Kumbh Mela when about 800 pilgrims were killed in a stampede of people moving toward the Ganges River.

- A video game for kids is based on the adventures of Hanuman, a Hindu god.

- The Madhya Pradesh province of India held a *Ramayana* festival in 2008 in which actors from six countries—Cambodia, Vietnam, Burma (Myanmar), Sri Lanka, Indonesia, and Laos—performed as Rama and Sita in their countries' own style and costumes.

- Hindus say the seven stars of the constellation Westerners call the Big Dipper are really seven wise men. Their long hair as it is being braided forms what non-Hindus call the Milky Way.

- Sanskrit is the basis for many European languages, including English.

- Some Hindus in India and other countries celebrate the New Year at different times. In southern India, Hindus begin their new year with the holiday of Ugadi, which occurs in March or April. Hindus in Nepal celebrate the New Year in March with the holiday of Nava Varsha.

- A few Indian gurus have traveled around the globe and acquired followers. One was A.C. Bhaktivedanta, whose young followers in the United States and Europe during the 1960s and 1970s became known for their "Hare Krishna" chants.

GLOSSARY

aum—sacred expression in Hindu worship

avatars—various physical forms in which a divine being may appear

bindi—small dot that Hindu priests place on the foreheads of people after worship in a mandir

Brahmin—highest or priestly caste in traditional Hindu societies

caste—social class of people according to ancient Hindu tradition

Dalits—Hindus without caste who traditionally performed the most undesirable jobs

devout—believing in and following religious traditions

dharma—person's duty in daily life

guru—teacher who offers spiritual wisdom and advice

icons—images of holy figures

karma—person's good and bad acts in life, which affect rebirth and the possibility of moksha

mandir—Hindu temple

mantras—prayers

meditate—relax one's mind and body using a regular program of mental exercise

moksha—salvation or release from the cycle of birth and rebirth

murtis—sacred images, often pictures or statues of gods or goddesses

puja—worship in a temple or a home

Puranas—folktales about the gods and ancient heroes

reincarnation—rebirth of a dead person's soul in a new body

samsara—wheel of life, representing the cycle of birth and rebirth

samskaras—16 rituals that mark important stages in a Hindu's life

Sanskrit—ancient, sacred language of Hinduism

sects—branches of a religion or other large group

sustainer—one who gives another the strength and energy to keep going

yoga—form of Hindu meditation that involves physical and mental exercise as ways to become closer to spiritual existence

FURTHER REFERENCE

Nonfiction

Barnes, Trevor. *Hinduism and Other Eastern Religions:
Worship, Festivals, and Ceremonies From Around the World.*
Boston: Kingfisher, 2005.

Ganeri, Anita. *Hindu Mandirs.* Chicago: Raintree, 2006.

Parker-Rock, Michelle. *Diwali: The Hindu Festival of Lights, Feasts,
and Family.* Berkeley Heights, N.J.: Enslow Publishers, 2004.

Fiction

Byng, Georgia. *Molly Moon's Hypnotic Time Travel Adventure.*
New York: HarperCollinsPublishers, 2005.

Johari, Harish. *How Parvati Won the Heart of Shiva.* Rochester, Vt.:
Bear Cub Books, 2004.

Whelan, Gloria. *Homeless Bird.* New York: HarperCollinsPublishers, 2000.

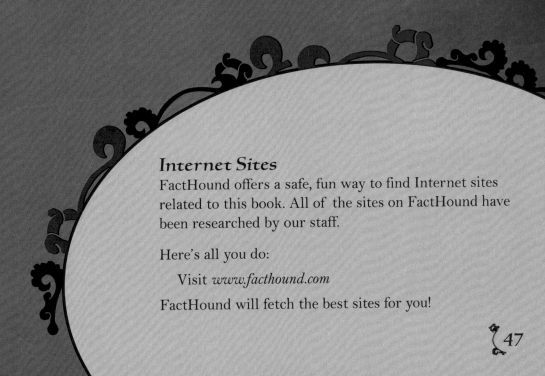

Internet Sites

FactHound offers a safe, fun way to find Internet sites
related to this book. All of the sites on FactHound have
been researched by our staff.

Here's all you do:

Visit *www.facthound.com*

FactHound will fetch the best sites for you!

INDEX

ABOUT THE AUTHOR

Natalie M. Rosinsky is the award-winning author of more than 100 publications. These include *Judaism*, books about 10 Native American tribes, *Write Your Own Myth*, and *Write Your Own Fable*. She lives and works in Mankato, Minnesota. Natalie earned graduate degrees from the University of Wisconsin-Madison and has been a high school teacher and college professor as well as a corporate trainer.